Animal Top Tens

The Ocean's Most Amazing Animals

Anita Ganeri

www.raintreepublishers.co.uk
Visit our website to find out more information about Raintree books.

To order:
☎ Phone 44 (0) 1865 888112
🗎 Send a fax to 44 (0) 1865 314091
💻 Visit the Raintree Bookshop at **www.raintreepublishers.co.uk** to browse our catalogue and order online

First published in Great Britain by Raintree, Halley Court, Jordan Hill, Oxford OX2 8EJ, part of Harcourt Education.
Raintree is a registered trademark of Harcourt Education Ltd.

Editorial: Nancy Dickmann and Catherine Veitch
Design: Victoria Bevan and Geoff Ward
Illustrations: Geoff Ward
Picture Research: Mica Brancic
Production: Victoria Fitzgerald

Originated by Modern Age
Printed and bound by CTPS (China Translation & Printing Services Ltd)

13-digit ISBN 978 1 4062 0920 4
12 11 10 09 08
10 9 8 7 6 5 4 3 2 1

British Library Cataloguing in Publication Data
Ganeri, Anita, 1961-
The Oceans' Most Amazing Animals.
(Animal top tens)
591.7'7
A full catalogue record for this book is available from the British Library.

Acknowledgements
The author and publisher are grateful to the following for permission to reproduce copyright material: ©Ardea pp. **16** (D. Parer & E. Parer-Cook), **24** (M. Watson); ©FLPA/Minden Pictures pp. **4, 11, 23**; ©FLPA/Panda Photo p. **26**; ©Getty p. **9** (Stephen Frink) [Ardea]; ©Getty Images p. **19** (Brian J. Skerry); ©Image Quest Marine pp. **14** (Carlos Villoch), **17** (Jez Tryner), **18** (Justin Marshall), **19** (Peter Herring), **25** (Mark Conlin-V&W); ©Image Quest Marine/2004 p. **15** (Tony Reavill); ©Image Quest Marine/2005 p. **27** (Masa Ushioda); ©OSF pp. **6** (Doug Perrine), **7** (Howard Hall), **8** (David B. Fleetham), **10** (Dave Fleetham), **12** (Max Gibbs); ©PA Photos/AP Photo p. **18** (Tsunemi Kubodera of the National Science Museum of Japan, HO).

Cover photograph of an orca breaching, reproduced with permission of Naturepl.com/Brandon Cole.

The publishers would like to thank Michael Bright for his assistance with the preparation of this book.

Every effort has been made to contact copyright holders of any material reproduced in this book. Any omissions will be rectified in subsequent printings if notice is given to the publishers.

Contents

Some words are printed in bold, **like this**. You can find out what they mean on page 31 in the Glossary.

The oceans

Over two-thirds of the Earth is covered in sea water. This lies in five oceans which contain 97 per cent of all of the world's water. In order of size, the five oceans are the Pacific, Atlantic, Indian, Southern (also known as the Antarctic Ocean), and Arctic. The Pacific is the largest ocean by far. It stretches almost halfway around the world. It is also the deepest ocean, plunging to 11 kilometres (6.8 miles) at its deepest point.

Thousands of amazing animals live in ocean habitats, such as coral reefs.

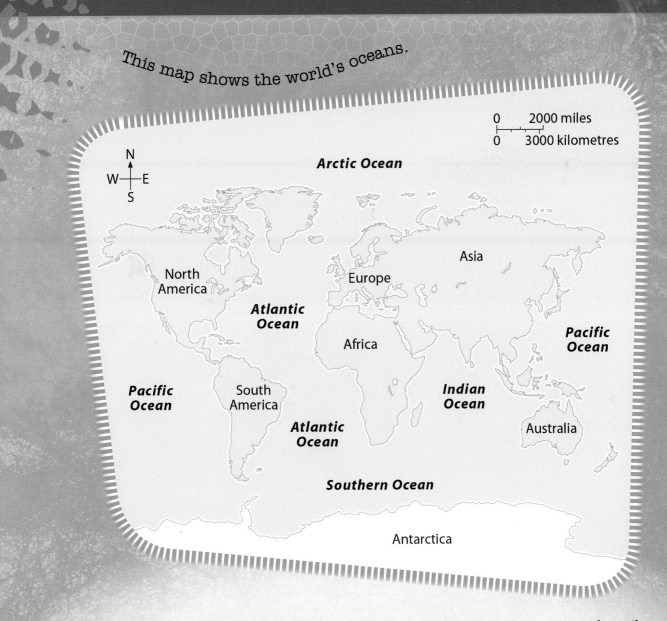

N
W E
S

0   2000 miles
0   3000 kilometres

Arctic Ocean

North America

Europe

Asia

Atlantic Ocean

Africa

Pacific Ocean

Pacific Ocean

South America

Indian Ocean

Atlantic Ocean

Australia

Southern Ocean

Antarctica

Together, the oceans form the largest **habitat** on Earth. They are home to a huge number and variety of animals, from tiny shrimps to enormous whales. Animals live in every part of the sea, from the surface water to the deep-sea bed. Some animals live in the open ocean; others live along the coast.

In each part of the ocean, animals have different conditions to cope with, such as increasing **water pressure** or lack of light or food. Many ocean animals have special features to help them survive in the conditions they live in.

Sailfish

Sailfish live near the surface of the sea. They feed on smaller fish, squid, and octopus. They get their name from their sail-like back **fins**. They raise their fins when they are threatened to make them look bigger and fiercer.

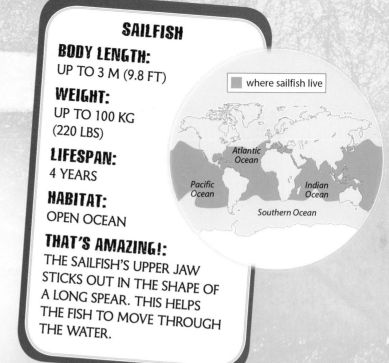

SAILFISH

BODY LENGTH:
UP TO 3 M (9.8 FT)

WEIGHT:
UP TO 100 KG
(220 LBS)

LIFESPAN:
4 YEARS

HABITAT:
OPEN OCEAN

THAT'S AMAZING!:
THE SAILFISH'S UPPER JAW STICKS OUT IN THE SHAPE OF A LONG SPEAR. THIS HELPS THE FISH TO MOVE THROUGH THE WATER.

where sailfish live

Atlantic Ocean
Pacific Ocean
Indian Ocean
Southern Ocean

Sailfish also use their sails to herd fish together. This makes the fish easier to catch.

When it is swimming very quickly, a sailfish's sail folds down to help with **streamlining**.

Predators and prey

In the open ocean, there is nowhere to hide from enemies. Prey animals have other ways of protecting themselves. Many small fish are silver and white so they are **camouflaged** in the water. Others wait until dark before coming to the surface to feed.

Streamlining

Open ocean **predators** cover vast distances in search of **prey.** The sailfish has a sleek, long body for fast swimming. It can reach speeds of over 110 kph (68 mph). This makes it the fastest fish in the sea.

Great white shark

The great white shark is the largest fish **predator** in the
sea. It feeds on fish, seals, sea lions, and dolphins. The
shark's colouring makes it difficult for **prey** to spot.
From above, its grey-blue back blends in with the water
beneath. From below, the white colour of its belly
blends in with the surface of the sea.

The great white shark's body is **streamlined** for swimming at speed.

GREAT WHITE SHARK

BODY LENGTH:
UP TO 7 M (22.9 FT)

WEIGHT:
UP TO 3 TONNES
(3.3 TONS)

LIFESPAN:
AROUND 15 YEARS

HABITAT:
OPEN OCEAN

THAT'S AMAZING!:
SHARK SKIN IS SO ROUGH
THAT PEOPLE ONCE USED
IT AS SANDPAPER.

Arctic Ocean

Atlantic
Ocean

Pacific
Ocean

Indian
Ocean

Southern Ocean

where great
white sharks live

Shark hunting

The great white shark's body is built for hunting. It uses sight, smell, and hearing to find prey. It uses its snout to pick up electrical signals given off by living things. Then the shark charges and bites. Its jaws are lined with sharp, jagged teeth. If prey is too big to eat in one go, the shark shakes its head from side to side, sawing off chunks of meat.

Orca

The orca, or killer whale, is a fast, sleek hunter. It kills and eats fish, sharks, squid, seals, and sea lions. The orca has striking black and white colouring. It swims among the shadows near the surface and takes its **prey** by surprise.

ORCA

BODY LENGTH:
5.5–9 M
(18–29.5 FT)

WEIGHT:
OVER 6 TONNES (6.6 TONS)

LIFESPAN:
30–50 YEARS

HABITAT:
OPEN OCEANS; COASTS

THAT'S AMAZING!:
THE ORCA HAS WHITE EYESPOTS ON BOTH SIDES OF ITS HEAD. THIS HELPS ORCAS TO SPOT EACH OTHER IN THE POD.

where orcas live

Atlantic Ocean

Pacific Ocean

Indian Ocean

Southern Ocean

Orcas are found in all of the world's oceans but like the colder water of the **polar** seas.

Teamwork

Orcas sometimes hunt in groups, driving fish towards the shore. Here the fish get trapped and are easy to catch. Other orcas attack **shoals** of herrings by slapping the shoal with their tails to stun or kill the fish. Orcas have also been seen knocking seals off the ice, or deliberately launching themselves on to the shore to catch sea lions.

Orcas live in family groups, called pods, of 5 to 30 whales.

Blue-ringed octopus

The tiny blue-ringed octopus lives along the coasts of Australia and the Pacific Islands. It lives in cracks in rocks and coral reefs. It has eight arms and a beak-like mouth.

The octopus's rings glow bright blue when it is about to bite.

Coral reefs

Coral reefs are the richest **habitat** in the sea. They are built by tiny animals, called coral polyps. The polyps use chemicals from sea water to build hard skeletons around their soft bodies. When the polyps die, their hard coral cases are left behind.

Deadly poison

The blue-ringed octopus is one of the most dangerous animals in the sea. Its saliva contains two kinds of **venom**. One is mild and is used for killing small crabs and shrimps for food. The other is used in self-defence and is so deadly that it could kill a person in minutes.

BLUE-RINGED OCTOPUS

BODY LENGTH:
UP TO 20 CM (8 IN)

WEIGHT:
UP TO 100 G
(0.22 LBS)

LIFESPAN:
2 YEARS

HABITAT:
SHALLOW WATER
ON CORAL REEFS AND
IN ROCK POOLS

THAT'S AMAZING!:
IF ONE OF THE OCTOPUS'S ARMS
GETS LOST OR DAMAGED, IT
CAN GROW A NEW ONE.

Arctic Ocean

Atlantic
Ocean

Pacific
Ocean

Indian
Ocean

Southern Ocean

where blue-ringed
octopuses live

Parrotfish

Parrotfish get their name from their bright colours and from their beak-like mouths. They use their mouths to scrape the tiny plants they feed on from the coral. As they feed, they bite off pieces of coral which they grind up with their flat teeth. The coral passes through the fishes' bodies and comes out at the other end as white coral sand.

Like parrots, parrotfish come in many colours – red, green, blue, pink, and yellow.

Sleeping habits

Parrotfish are active by day. At night, some kinds of parrotfish burrow into the sand or hide in cracks in the coral. Others make a slimy coat around their bodies, like a sleeping bag. This is thought to hide their smell. It is then difficult for night **predators**, such as moray eels, to find and eat the fish.

sleeping bag

PARROTFISH

BODY LENGTH:
UP TO 1.2 M (3.94 FT)

WEIGHT:
UP TO 20 KG (44 LBS)

LIFESPAN:
UP TO 7 YEARS

HABITAT:
CORAL REEFS

THAT'S AMAZING!:
PARROTFISH HELP TO KEEP REEFS HEALTHY. THE PLANTS THEY FEED ON CAN HARM THE CORAL IF THEY ARE LEFT TO GROW.

where parrotfish live

Pacific Ocean

Indian Ocean

Southern Ocean

A parrotfish sleeping bag takes about half an hour to build and break out of.

Giant clam

The largest and heaviest shellfish in the sea is the enormous giant clam. It lives on coral reefs in the Indian and Pacific Oceans. Its thick hard shell is made up of two parts which protect the soft, fleshy body of the clam.

GIANT CLAM

SHELL LENGTH:
UP TO 1.3 M (4.2 FT)

WEIGHT:
UP TO 300 KG (660 LBS)

LIFESPAN:
MORE THAN 100 YEARS

HABITAT:
CORAL REEFS

THAT'S AMAZING!:
THE EMPTY SHELL OF A GIANT CLAM, AFTER THE CLAM HAS DIED, IS OFTEN HOME TO OTHER CREATURES, SUCH AS CORALS, SEA ANEMONES AND SPONGES.

where giant clams live

Atlantic Ocean

Pacific Ocean

Indian Ocean

Southern Ocean

The giant clam's colourful body can be seen between the two shells.

Giant clam garden

The clam's body has two tubes, called siphons. It sucks water in through one of the tubes, and filters out tiny plants and animals. Then it squirts the water out through the other tube. But the clam gets most of its food from the tiny **algae** that grow in its body. In return, the algae get a safe place to live.

Once a giant clam has settled into place on the reef, it will not move for the rest of its life.

Giant squid

The giant squid lives in all of the world's oceans. But it is very rarely seen because it lives so deep in the water. A squid swims by sucking in water, then suddenly squeezing it out again. This is called jet propulsion.

GIANT SQUID

BODY LENGTH:
OVER 15 M (49.2 FT)

WEIGHT:
OVER A TONNE (TON)

LIFESPAN:
50–80 YEARS

HABITAT:
DEEP SEA

THAT'S AMAZING!:
GIANT SQUID FLOAT UPRIGHT IN THE OCEAN BECAUSE THEIR BODIES ARE FILLED WITH CHEMICALS WHICH ARE LIGHTER THAN SEAWATER.

where giant squid live

Atlantic Ocean

Pacific Ocean

Indian Ocean

Southern Ocean

The giant squid is one of the world's longest **invertebrates**.

A squid's arms and tentacles are lined with hundreds of powerful suckers.

Deep-sea fishing

A giant squid is well suited for catching its **prey** in the deep sea. Its eyes are the size of footballs to help it see in the dark water. It has eight arms and two extra-long **tentacles**. Squids use their tentacles to catch their prey of deep-sea fish and squid. Then they tear into the prey with their razor-sharp beaks. A squid's enemies are deep-sea sharks and sperm whales. Some sperm whales have been found with squid remains in their stomachs or scars from squid suckers on their skin.

Deep-sea angler fish

The deeper you go down in the oceans, the colder and darker it is. The **water pressure** is crushing and there is very little food. Despite this, some amazing animals, such as the deep-sea angler fish, have **adapted** to deep-sea living.

DEEP-SEA ANGLER FISH

BODY LENGTH:
UP TO 1 M (ABOUT 3 FT)

WEIGHT:
UP TO 50 KG (110 LBS)

LIFESPAN:
1–3 YEARS

HABITAT:
DEEP SEA

THAT'S AMAZING!:
SOME ANGLER FISH ARE COVERED IN LONG SPINES TO HELP THEM FIND PREY MOVING IN THE DARK WATER.

Arctic Ocean

Atlantic Ocean

Pacific Ocean

Indian Ocean

Southern Ocean

where deep-sea angler fish live

For **camouflage** in the pitch-black water, deep-sea angler fish are dark brown or black.

Fishing for food

Deep-sea angler fish use light to trap food. A long, thin fin like a fishing rod grows over the fish's head. It has a bulb of glowing bacteria on the end, which acts like bait. Small fish think the light is a meal and swim straight into the angler's mouth.

Making light

Over half of deep-sea fish make light to trap **prey**, confuse **predators** and communicate. Some do this by **chemical reactions** inside their bodies. Others contain billions of tiny, glowing bacteria.

Deep-sea angler fish have huge mouths. These are lined with long, curved teeth.

Gulper eel

The gulper eel is a very long, black, deep-sea fish. It has tiny eyes at the end of its snout and a small, reddish light at the tip of its long, whip-like tail. It uses its tail for movement and its light to tempt **prey**.

Gulper eels live up to 3 kilometres (1.8 miles) down in the sea.

Eating machine

Food is scarce in the deep sea so gulper eels have **adapted** to make the most of any food they find. The gulper eel hangs in the water, waiting for prey to swim past. It has a huge mouth which it can open wide like a fishing net. This lets the eel swallow animals much larger than itself.

GULPER EEL

BODY LENGTH:
UP TO 2 M (6.6 FT)

WEIGHT:
UNKNOWN

LIFESPAN:
UNKNOWN

HABITAT:
DEEP SEA

THAT'S AMAZING!:
GULPER EELS ARE ALSO KNOWN AS PELICAN EELS BECAUSE THEIR LOWER JAWS LOOK LIKE A PELICAN'S POUCH.

where gulper eels live

Atlantic Ocean

Pacific Ocean

Indian Ocean

Southern Ocean

Green turtle

Each year, thousands of green turtles leave their feeding grounds in Brazil. They swim over 2,000 kilometres (1,242 miles) to lay their eggs on tiny Ascension Island in the middle of the Atlantic Ocean. These amazing animals may find their way by smell or by the stars but no one knows for certain.

Migration

Many sea animals, including seals, whales, lobsters and turtles, make long journeys between their **breeding** and feeding grounds. This is called **migration**. It allows them to enjoy the best weather and food supplies in each place.

The female turtles dig holes in the sand with their back flippers.

Nesting beaches

Female turtles lay about 100-200 eggs in holes on the sandy beach. They cover the eggs with sand and go back to the sea. When the baby turtles hatch, they head straight to the sea.

Many baby turtles are eaten by crabs and gulls on their way to the sea.

GREEN TURTLE

BODY LENGTH:
UP TO 1.5 M (4.9 FT)

WEIGHT:
UP TO 300 KGS
(660 LBS)

LIFESPAN:
UP TO 80 YEARS

HABITAT:
WARM, SHALLOW WATER

THAT'S AMAZING!:
GREEN TURTLES ARE NAMED AFTER THE GREENISH COLOUR OF THEIR SKIN.

where green turtles live

Atlantic
Ocean

Pacific
Ocean

Indian
Ocean

Southern Ocean

Animals in danger

Many ocean animals are in danger of dying out. When an animal dies out, it is said to be **extinct.** Animals are dying out because of overfishing, hunting, and because their **habitat** is being damaged by pollution.

Millions of tonnes of fish are caught for food every year. But some fish are being taken from the sea faster than they can **breed,** grow and restock. Today, overfishing is a serious problem. Southern bluefin tuna live in the Indian Ocean where they are caught in large numbers.

So many bluefin tuna fish are being caught that soon there may not be many left.

There are fewer than 400 Mediterranean monk seals left in the wild.

Sea **mammals** are also in danger. The Mediterranean monk seal is one of the rarest animals in the world. It is nearly extinct. In the past the seals were hunted for their meat and skins. Today, noisy, crowded holiday resorts are being built on seals' breeding sites. This means that the seals are breeding less.

Today, **conservation** groups are working hard to save these amazing animals.

Animal facts and figures

There are millions of different kinds of animals living all over the world. The place where an animal lives is called its **habitat**. Animals have special features, such as wings, claws, and fins. These features allow animals to survive in their habitats. Which animal do you think is the most amazing?

SAILFISH

BODY LENGTH:
UP TO 3 M (9.8 FT)

WEIGHT:
UP TO 100 KG (220 LBS)

LIFESPAN:
4 YEARS

HABITAT:
OPEN OCEAN

THAT'S AMAZING!:
THE SAILFISH'S UPPER JAW STICKS OUT IN THE SHAPE OF A LONG SPEAR. THIS HELPS THE FISH TO MOVE THROUGH THE WATER.

GREAT WHITE SHARK

BODY LENGTH:
UP TO 7 M (22.9 FT)

WEIGHT:
UP TO 3 TONNES (3.3 TONS)

LIFESPAN:
AROUND 15 YEARS

HABITAT:
OPEN OCEAN

THAT'S AMAZING!:
SHARK SKIN IS SO ROUGH THAT PEOPLE ONCE USED IT AS SANDPAPER.

ORCA

BODY LENGTH:
6.5–8 M (21.3–26.2 FT)

WEIGHT:
OVER 6 TONNES (6.6 TONS)

LIFESPAN:
30–50 YEARS

HABITAT:
OPEN OCEANS; COASTS

THAT'S AMAZING!:
THE ORCA HAS WHITE EYESPOTS ON BOTH SIDES OF ITS HEAD. THIS HELPS ORCAS TO SPOT EACH OTHER IN THE POD.

BLUE-RINGED OCTOPUS

BODY LENGTH:
UP TO 20 CM (8 IN)

WEIGHT:
UP TO 100 G (0.22 LBS)

LIFESPAN:
2 YEARS

HABITAT:
SHALLOW WATER ON CORAL REEFS AND IN ROCK POOLS

THAT'S AMAZING!:
IF ONE OF THE OCTOPUS'S ARMS GETS LOST OR DAMAGED, IT CAN GROW A NEW ONE.

PARROTFISH

BODY LENGTH:
UP TO 1.2 M (3.94 FT)

WEIGHT:
UP TO 20 KG (44 LBS)

LIFESPAN:
UP TO 7 YEARS

HABITAT:
CORAL REEFS

THAT'S AMAZING!:
PARROTFISH HELP TO KEEP REEFS HEALTHY. THE PLANTS THEY FEED ON CAN HARM THE CORAL IF THEY ARE LEFT TO GROW.

GIANT CLAM

SHELL LENGTH:
UP TO 1.3 M (4.2 FT)

WEIGHT:
UP TO 300 KG (660 LBS)

LIFESPAN:
MORE THAN 100 YEARS

HABITAT:
CORAL REEFS

THAT'S AMAZING!:
THE EMPTY SHELL OF A GIANT CLAM, AFTER THE CLAM HAS DIED, IS OFTEN HOME TO OTHER CREATURES, SUCH AS CORALS, SEA ANEMONES AND SPONGES.

GIANT SQUID

BODY LENGTH:
OVER 15 M (49.2 FT)

WEIGHT:
OVER A TONNE (TON)

LIFESPAN:
50–80 YEARS

HABITAT:
DEEP SEA

THAT'S AMAZING!:
GIANT SQUID FLOAT UPRIGHT IN THE OCEAN BECAUSE THEIR BODIES ARE FILLED WITH CHEMICALS WHICH ARE LIGHTER THAN SEAWATER.

DEEP-SEA ANGLER FISH

BODY LENGTH:
UP TO 1 M (ABOUT 3 FT)

WEIGHT:
UP TO 50 KG (110 LBS)

LIFESPAN:
1–3 YEARS

HABITAT:
DEEP SEA

THAT'S AMAZING!:
SOME ANGLER FISH ARE COVERED IN LONG SPINES TO HELP THEM FIND PREY MOVING IN THE DARK WATER.

GULPER EEL

BODY LENGTH:
UP TO 2 M (6.6 FT)

WEIGHT:
UNKNOWN

LIFESPAN:
UNKNOWN

HABITAT:
DEEP SEA

THAT'S AMAZING!:
GULPER EELS ARE ALSO KNOWN AS PELICAN EELS BECAUSE THEIR LOWER JAWS LOOK LIKE A PELICAN'S POUCH.

GREEN TURTLE

BODY LENGTH:
UP TO 1.5 M (4.9 FT)

WEIGHT:
UP TO 300 KGS (660 LBS)

LIFESPAN:
UP TO 80 YEARS

HABITAT:
WARM, SHALLOW WATER

THAT'S AMAZING!:
GREEN TURTLES ARE NAMED AFTER THE GREENISH COLOUR OF THEIR SKIN.

Find out more

Books to read

Living Things: Adaptation, Holly Wallace (Heinemann Library, 2001)

Living Things: Survival and Change, Holly Wallace (Heinemann Library, 2001)

The Blue Planet, Alastair Fothergill, (BBC Books, 2001)

Websites

http://www.bbc.co.uk/nature/reallywild
Type in the name of the animal you want to learn about and find a page with lots of facts, figures, and pictures.

http://animals.nationalgeographic.com/animals
This site has information on the different groups of animals, stories of survival in different habitats, and stunning photo galleries to search through.

http://animaldiversity.ummz.umich.edu
A website run by the University of Michigan which has a huge encyclopedia of animals to search through.

http://www.mnh.si.edu
The website of the Smithsonian National Museum of Natural History, which has one of the largest natural history collections in the world.

Zoo sites
Many zoos around the world have their own websites which tell you about the animals they keep, where they come from, and how they are looked after.

Glossary

adapted when an animal has special features that help it to survive in its habitat

algae very simple plants that live in water

breed when an animal makes babies with another animal

camouflage when an animal has special colours or markings which help to hide it in its habitat

chemical reaction when different chemicals mix together

conservation saving and protecting threatened animals and habitats

extinct when a kind of animal dies out forever

fin part of a fish's body that is used for swimming and steering

habitat place where an animal lives and feeds

invertebrates animals without backbones inside their bodies

mammal animal that has fur or hair and feeds its babies on milk

migration long journey made by some animals to find a better place to breed or feed in

polar areas around the North and South Poles

predator animal that hunts and kills other animals for food

prey animals that are hunted and killed by other animals for food

reptile animal with scaly skin that lays eggs on land

shoal large group of fish

streamlined having a long, smooth shape for cutting through the air or water

tentacle long part of some sea animals' bodies which is used for feeding and gripping

venom poison from an animal

water pressure weight of the water pressing down from above

Index